AF601666

Colin Read || Reade Collins
contact@readecollinsart.com
colin@artsandminds.info

Other Works by Colin Read / Reade Collins

Poetry Collections

"52 Days, 63 Poems"

"The Spaces We Inhabit"

"Memory and the Construction of Histories"

Music

search by title or "Reade Collins" via most streaming services

"Lo-Fi Synthetics for Film and Video"

"Music for 6 Pianos and 1 Orchestra"

"Fuck the Flower Power Child"

"Audio Concrete"

mal de débarquement

Tue, 2015/08/11- 17:24

circadian
arrhythmia
its concrete and abstract
essence
comprehends
the existential
metaphor
of my being

mal de mer
mal de débarquement
mal de vivre...

Drive

(https://youtu.be/nrBXkUBogd4)

This is my world
I am encapsulated within
Mesmerised by the
Regularity
Rhythmic
Repetition
The passing by
Of the road
Of my life
Who
I was
and
Where
I was
Disappears
With each exchange

Rubber and bitumen –
The tyre meets the road
Osmosis
The outside
Meets
The inside
The balance
Of
The Universe
Is maintained
But I
Have become
Less

Attachment Theory

Mon, 2013/05/20 - 12:25

Mother
I am here beneath the piano stool
Am I hidden
Or do you see me
As you hold my brother
In your arms
And whisper
Your love?

Maybe
I had been too often the angry child
Unsettled
With the un-comprehending rage
Of sibling rivalry.

But a desire
To be held
And whispered to
To be held
And told
To be held
And to hold
Was then and there

Was it only a second
An instance
A moment?
It has travelled with me
Forever since.

As the slightest shifting
In the second of an arc
Removes the destination
With increasing separation
In each step of the journey
So, too, the need increases
With each passing second
In this existential momentum.

But a desire
To be held
And whispered to
To be held
And told
To be held
And to hold
Is now and here

Its incrementing grab and stab
Is exponential in my heart.

The catch is
If I ask for my redemption
It has not been given
Unbidden
Of you,
And there will always be doubt...

Each Minor Fear

Fri, 2013/04/05 - 07:28

Each minor fear
Each life taboo
Defines our years
In private truths
Each painted lie
A rationale
Of feigned disguise
And carnival

We dig each hole
And bury deep
Within our soul
We pray to keep
Our hearts interred
In catacomb
Of life deferred
To monochrome

Two Sleeps to Go

Thu, 2012/04/26 - 09:47

We have only two sleeps to go
Or so the brothers tell me
They share a special bond, fraternally
(These brothers - they are twins, see)
Hypnos and Thanatos.

One sleep I am glad to know
The other sleep will fell me
And there I'll lie beyond, eternally
When finally it wins me -
"Vanitas vanitatum Omnia Vanitas!"

I stand with Yalom by my side
He is teaching me to stare
At the sun in all its terror
The unspoken is our common ground
Our sure and shared finality.

And in my night I can confide
With the moon - it's always there
To share the burdens of my error
Within each painting's strokes are found

The essence of my enmities
Are cause for fear of grace
I steel my focus and begin
Despondence derides my every day
Insistent to defeat me.

In the presence of mine enemies
I pause and clear a space
I feel their locus from within
As confidants to guide me on my way...
I shift and rise to greet me.

A Poem of Avoidance

Wed, 2011/11/16 - 08:06

There is more to do
Than I can possibly do
And I can only do
What I can do -
No more.

My inner world
Establishes that all is more
Than can be done
And I forget
That I can eat the elephant
(One mouthful at a time).

I am plagued and terrorized
By the guilt
Of my inaction
And the fear
Of taking the first step
Precludes the possibility
Of getting anywhere.

I, Machine

Wed, 2011/09/28 - 15:15

Descartes' Cartesian Dualism
Gave me a mind
Separate to the machine
Sure, this is my brain -
"Mais, je pense, donc je suis"
The machine may stop
But the mind... ah! the mind...

I, machine
Oligodendrocytes
Axonal electrical tape
Breaking down
Demyelinating
The machine starts to fall apart
Each Node of Ranvier
Loses its identity
To gaping chasms and fissures

What were once sparks
Driven with velocity
On the straight and narrow
To a certain synaptic potential
Are now sluggish and unpredictable
Powder flashes

**Wildfire erupts throughout the glia
Half my consciousness
Is overcome by
A tsunami of blood
Suffocation and infarction
Someone else's arm has been
Attached to the left side of my body
And I, machine,
Am fucked!**

**Descartes
I saw your fMRI
You were thinking at the time -
Lit up and sparkling
In all your neuronal glory**

Saturday Mornings

Wed, 2011/05/18 - 12:06

Saturday mornings
It's newspapers and coffee
Toast and jam and tea
We sit on the back porch
And a song constantly plays
In my mind
The words silently forming their shape
On my lips
It is a love song
And while I'm not fully aware of it
It shapes my sense of completeness

The Little Proofs

Sat, 2011/05/14 - 21:33

Leave truth to the philosophers

I only know
What I think I know
And even that
Is reliant on my memory

I mean
What is the truth
Of my history?
The actuality
Of my past?

The reality
Of what has been
Is circumscribed
And defined
By the interpretations
Of the things I recall

I only know that
This is how I have been
By the conviction
Of my recollections
And the little proofs
Of the memorabilia
Gathered together
In each event -

Flotsam and jetsam
Of my presence
And the small, shared
Reciprocal imprinting
Of our coexistence

She Visits Me

Sun, 2011/03/27 - 15:44

My sense of leftness
Has lost its potency

There is the time of the world around me
There is the time of my world inside me
There is the time of history behind me
There is the time (stood still) of the aged care facility
I now spend my time in
There is the time (an eternity - or so it seems) of waiting for the future
That will be

Although they are enmeshed and entwined
They don't synchronise anymore
I cannot tell which is the one
I need to believe
Which is reality
Which is the memory
Which is the dream.

Somewhere I sense that she has died
Maybe four or five years ago
Maybe last week
Maybe tomorrow
My damaged mind
Refuses to let me know
To reassure me
To convince me one way or the other

As a fact
I think she was here
Only last night

My arm was trembling
And full of pins and needles
And she was there
To comfort me
To reassure me
That if it was still a trouble tomorrow
We could always make an appointment
And drive to the doctors

That would have to be in the car
I'm going to have to sell
Two years ago
And arthritis
Refuses to let me steer
Without the pain of fear

And she couldn't drive
That car -
We no longer owned it
And she had died

I know at times
I can be a grumpy old shit
But she brings me
Joy, happiness, peace, reassurance and clarity
Every time
She visits me

Ashes

Tue, 2011/01/18 - 11:05

Ashes to ashes
Dust to dust
Atoms to atoms
Rust to rust

I believe that I touch
I believe that I see
I observe and I trust
All is all - as should be

Confined to a present
Determined by past
Juggernaut to a future
In paradox cast

Emotions qua objects
Perceptions qua truth
Metaphysics qua physics
Moribus qua ruth

An Instance of the Everyday

Sat, 2010/09/04 - 21:15

An autumn leaf
Falls
The metaphysical clock
Marks the point
Pre-set as an awakening alarm
Signalling the appointed time
When this small miracle is to occur
The confluence of this mighty clock's gears
and cogs
Dictate that I am to be present
When this leaf and branch
Repeat the annual expectation
Of their deciduous inheritance

(Or maybe I just happened to be there
When a gust of wind
And quiver of the branch
Caused the leaf
To fall -
I mean, it had to happen sometime)

Never-the-less,
I watch
The path the leaf takes
As it descends -
Breeze, thermal and atmosphere -
All in accord
With its own unique leafy aerodynamics -
Play keepings off
With its gravity bound
Inevitability.

Suddenly
A brilliant shaft of light -
A ray of sunlight
That has found a clear path
Through the dappling
Overhead canopy -
Intercepts the leaf's
Vacillating trace.

The impact is foudroyant
And I am outside the scene.
In less time than a thought
I am whipped through a complete
360o multi-camera sequence
Separated and orbiting,
I am witness to myself and the leaf,
The leaf and myself.

Unknowingly, I have joined the chorus Of
every magnificat
Spontaneously drawn to the lips
Of all those before me
And all those to come
Who have been encompassed
And transported
By an instance of the everyday.

Subsequent to this moment of infinity The
leaf continues its wavering flight Until it
settles on the moist and cushioned
collection
Of those that have gone before
And are now adding themselves
In self-decompositional sacrifice
To the humus of the future.

A blackbird -
Yellow beak at the ready -
Hops and pecks, hops and pecks
Through the mulchy dregs
Seeking some unwitting worm
Who, unbidden and unknowing
Will be transformed from
Composting assistant
To blackbird dinner
In the coincidence of location and beak.

Wet
(Lay Me Down in a Bed of Water)
("Reade Collins" on Apple Music or Spotify)

Sun, 2010/08/29 - 16:42

**I take a sip
Crystal clarity
Belies the richness
And multitude
Each drop contains
Take the lifetimes required
To count the total
H2O molecules held within
The history of its cycles
Encompasses all histories
And I may savour
The taste
Of all that has been
Both the glorious and the banal
In each mouthful**

Trying To Recall

(The Events at the end of Another Perfect Day)

Sun, 2010/08/08 - 12:46

Blood
Constant and ever present,
Unacknowledged in its gravid potential
To contain hope for a life
Long and fruitful
To offer insecurity and fear
When vitiated,
To bring conclusion
At the ceasing of the pattern -
Systole... diastole... systole... diastole...
The internal lifelong beating
Of the rhythm
We have danced to
All these years

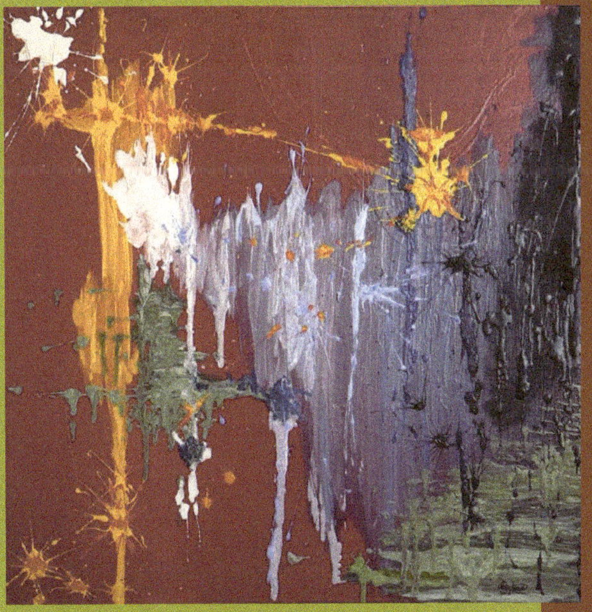

Sanguine
Is the colour
I perceive
When I close my eyes
And stare at the sun
Now setting

I am trying to recall
(The events at the end
Of another perfect day)
But they are fractured
And incomplete
Broad brushstrokes
Of significant happenings
Meld
With the minutiae
Of the banal

I hope for a detailed memoir
Giving rise to a transcendent contentment
As the list of the day
Is checked off one event at a time
(Where musings
Of this little history
Would give rise
To a divine and satiated pleasure
Replete in the perfection
Of each action that has
Lead to this singular point)

But instead
There is a flooding of colours -
The blinding core of the sun
White
The clouds paying homage to its western passage
Yellow... orange... pink...
The oceans and the sky
Blue
The trees and the fields
Green
The approaching night
Black

And though
It might not seem so
To any casual observer,
There is a
Beautiful congruence here

Red Flag
(https://youtu.be/LUQRURxO23Q)

Sun, 2010/07/25 - 15:50

My eye
Keeps on gravitating
Back to the red flag
But there is so much
Else to see -
So much movement
And vitality
In this point of view -
Overt and covert,
Revealed and held secret,
Declared and whispered

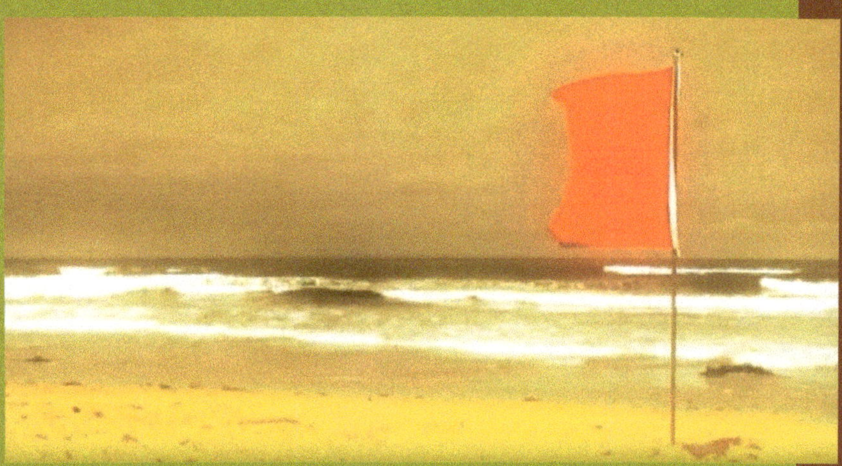

I try to force my eye
To wander
And rest -

Wander and rest -
The ocean
(Each wave)
The sky
(Each cloud)
The sand
(Each grain)
The wind
(Each breath)
But that damned
Red flag
Holds
Distracts
Demands

There is everything else to be seen here
But I can't get past the red flag...

In The Gutter -
Leaf Like My Loveheart

Thu, 2006/01/12 - 09:58

Dear Diary -
"...leaf
like my loveheart
lies
on a bed
of gravel and bluestone
only time will see it
weather
and wither
into
the detritus of this autumnal love...
decompose to recompose
...compost for a new spring growth..."

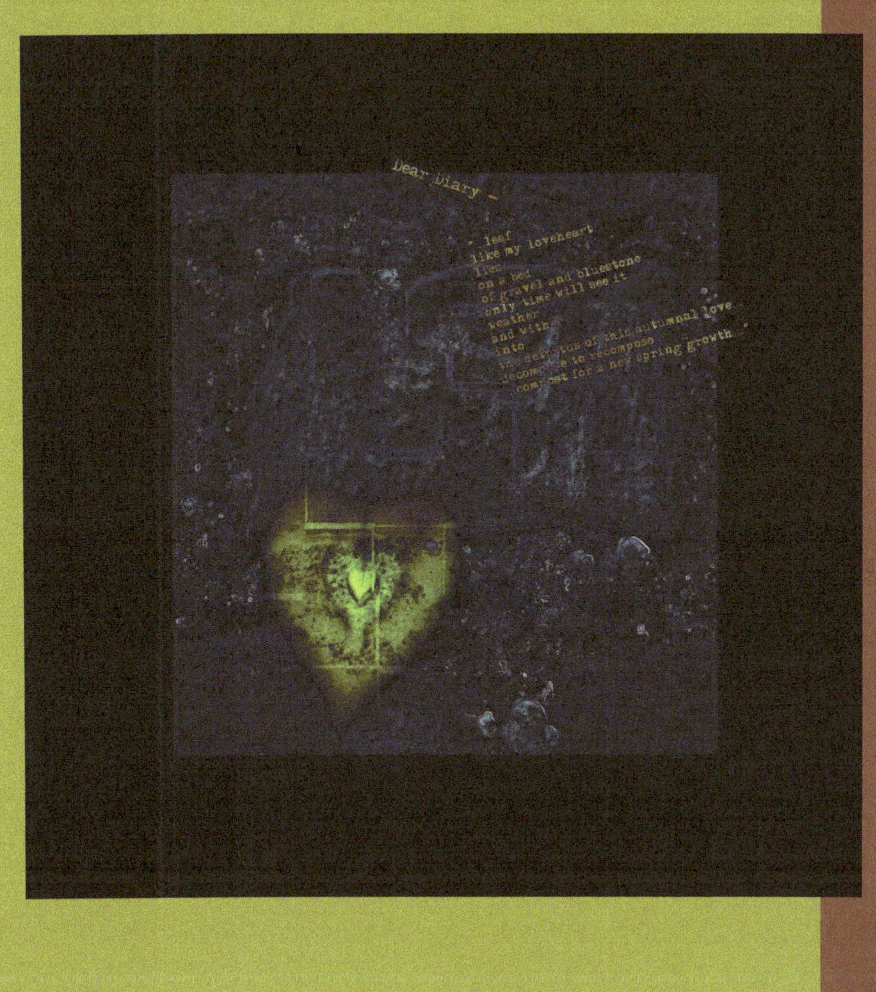
Dear Diary –
" leaf
like my loveheart
lies
on a bed
of gravel and bluestone
only time will see it
weather
and with
into
of this autumnal love.
to recompose
for a new spring growth. "

The Glove and The Jelly Fish

Wed, 2010/06/23 - 08:12

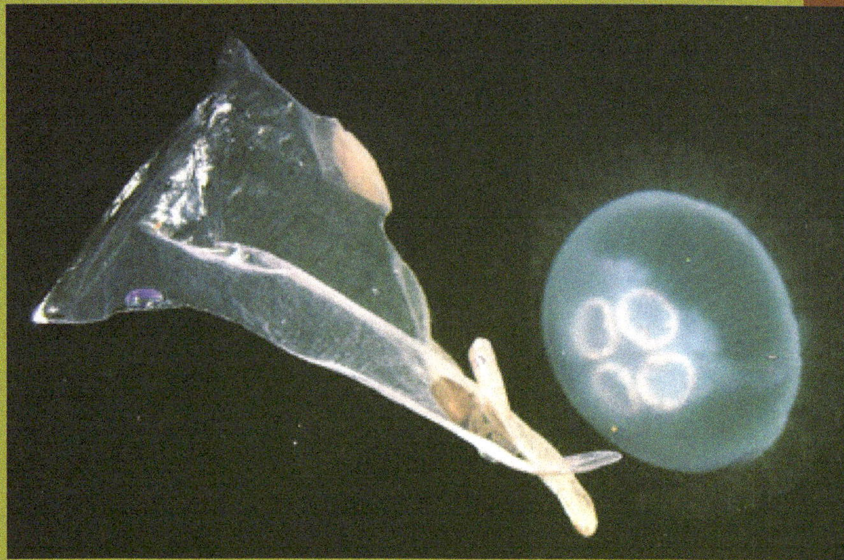

"Jelly Fish! Jelly Fish!
Come with me
We'll float together
Out to the sea
We'll go with the ebb
And the flow of each day
And let the currents
Determine our way

From the troughs to the crests
In perpetual motion
We'll ride the great waves
From ocean to ocean
Recording our journeys
In sinusoid traces
We'll visit far seaports
And exotic places"

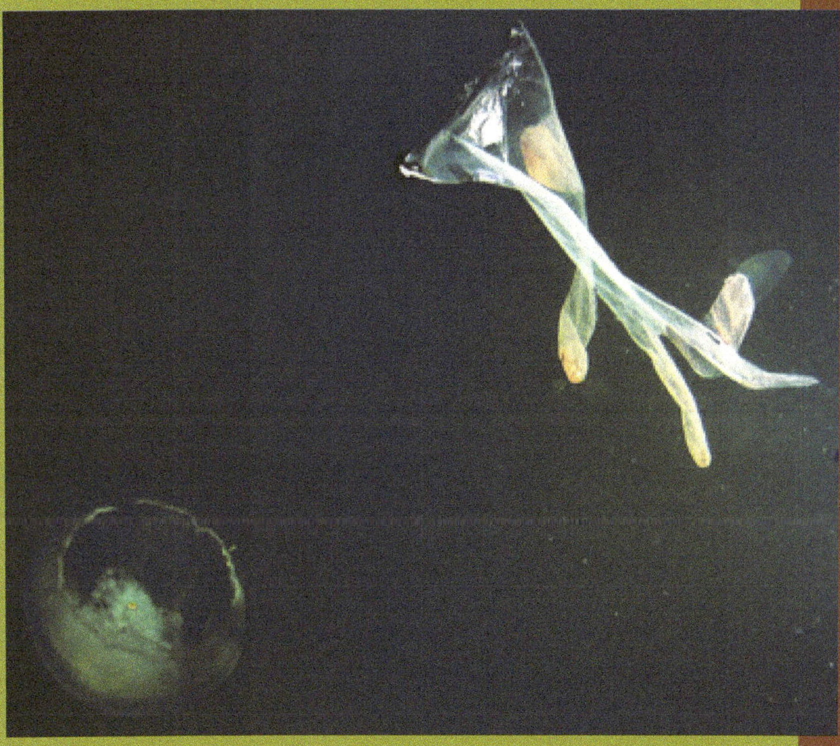

**"Oh, Glove! Dear, Glove!
Can't you see
That this relationship
Never can be?
For relying entirely
On predestination
May lead us to boredom
And exasperation**

**You dream that adventure
Will happen by chance -
Serendipitous wonder
In each circumstance -
And though it sounds tempting
I can't call it love
For I am a jellyfish
And you are a glove"**

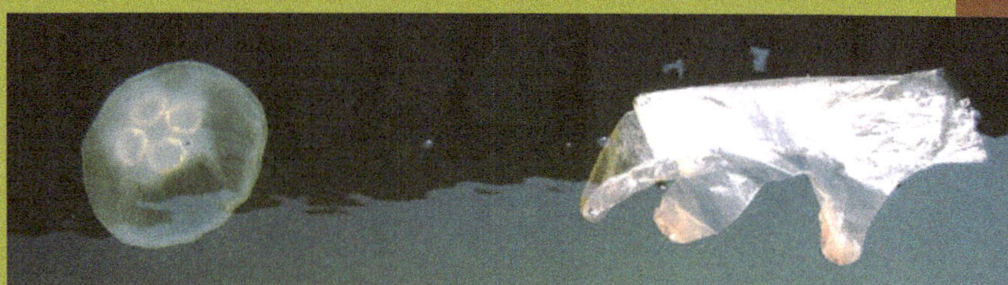

In Kapitsa's N

Fri, 2010/06/04 - 10:31

I am encapsulated
In Kapitsa's N[1]
Today
I try to keep a count
6.8 Giga+
And rising[2]

I perceive myself
In this fraction
1 of those
Arriving[3]

Journeying
And
Departing

As the denominator
Grows with
Exponential inevitability
This numerator
Is represented in
A diminishing
Point

In the glowing instances
Of data visualisations[4]

The beauty holds us captive
And we fail to witness
The moment
Of our own
Disappearing

---

1. https://en.wikipedia.org/wiki/World_population#Mathematical_approximations
2. http://www.worldometers.info/population/
3. http://www.worldometers.info/
4. https://www.bbc.co.uk/programmes/articles/3cWncg5C339NZ5XkBSQqyGN/numbers-game-the-artists-making-waves-with-big-data

---

I Can Only Remember Her Legs

(https://youtu.be/huCBXI-wUK8)

Mon, 2010/05/24 - 17:32

"We are
Passion and lust
And love -
Beyond -
We burn"
you said
"Our chemistry
Is that of
Spontaneity
And combustion"

This fire
Consumed
But was soon
Consumed
The Second Law
Of Thermodynamics
Overtook us in entropy
And found its balance
In the equilibrium
Of cooled indifference

Still, a kindling
Of our burning
Remains
But its fire
Overwhelms me
And I am loath
To acknowledge it
For it flames into
My recollecting
And when I try
I can only remember
Her legs

Kangaroo

Fri, 2010/05/21 - 12:08

Dry and desiccated
The heart conceals
The life contained
All around
Are our precious borders
Massaged and pummelled
To the edge
Of erosion
By the insistence
Of the ocean

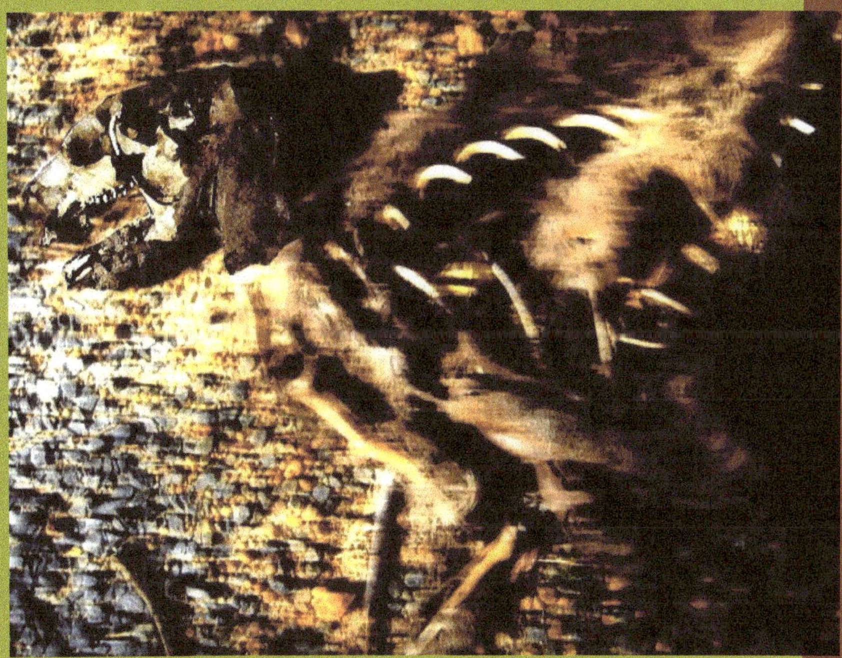

We have gouged
Our scars of transportation
From coast to coast to coast
Like reminders of self-harm
Their cross-hatching
Brings light and shade
To the monotony
Of our journeying

"Look, kids!
There's another one!
See how many we can count
Along the way..."

We plummet on
Reckoning up the tally
Occasionally
Nature is embedded
In an impact of
Time and place
Held within a moment
That seems to last forever
We totter on the precipice of
Synchronicity and fatality
And unwittingly
Yield our contribution
To the roadside
Memorials of decay

Bra On A Barbed Wire Fence

Tue, 2010/05/018 - 08:33

Puberty
Was quietly brooding
Self consciously

I stumbled
Uncoordinated
Through the surprise
Of growth spurts
And new
Obsessions

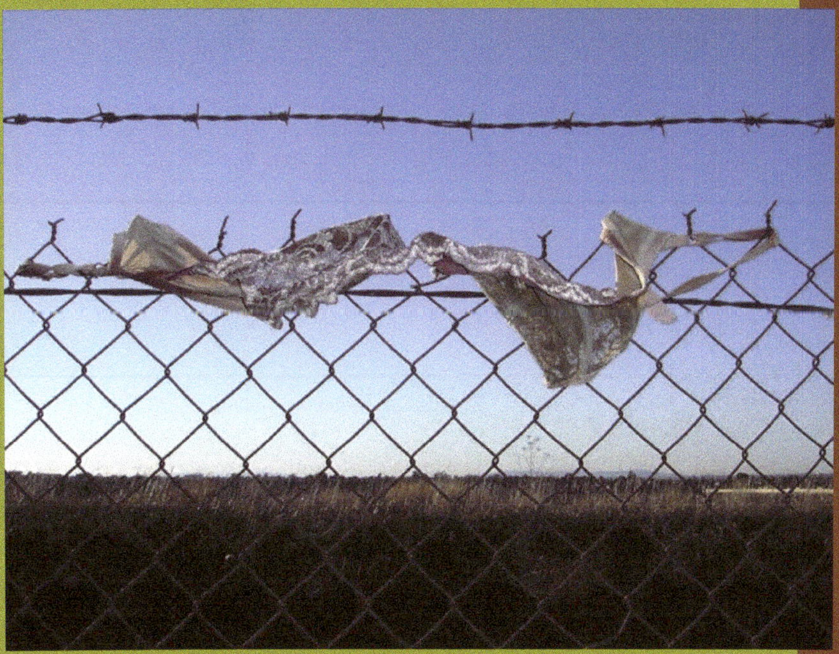

Back then,
What had been
The susurration
Of women's voices
Had become a roar
("I am woman!
Hear me...")
And the colours
Of this war's pennons
Were those
Of burning bras

Nearly 50 years since
I stumble across
A bra
On a barbed wire fence
All softness
And lace
Enmeshed in
Pike and barb
And wonder at
The prequel
To this
Mise en scene

Things That Burn - Burning Desires Series - "You Are Special - Teddy"

(https://youtu.be/EAmWPe9yTOM)

Thu, 2010/05/13 - 10:53

That was the end
It's not too clear now
All smiles and laughter
Nervously camouflaging the inevitable
Still it hit

With the force
Of the unexpected
And dragged me under
A juggernaut driven mercilessly
By a savaging pack
Of black dogs
And all that remained
Was a testament to the death

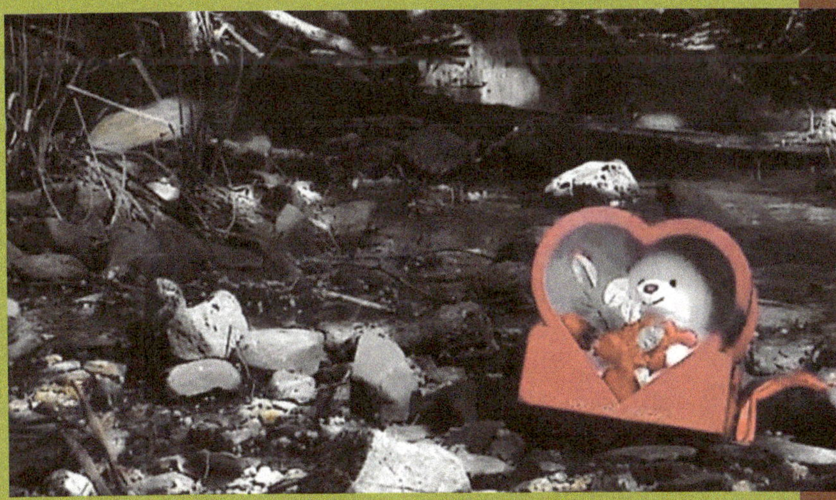

"You Are Special"
Mmm...
Not so much
Anymore

All things suffer
Entropy
Fire burns all desires
The ashes
Dissolve and dissipate
As forgotten
History

Her Arm Silhouette.

Sun, 2008/05/25 - 13:20

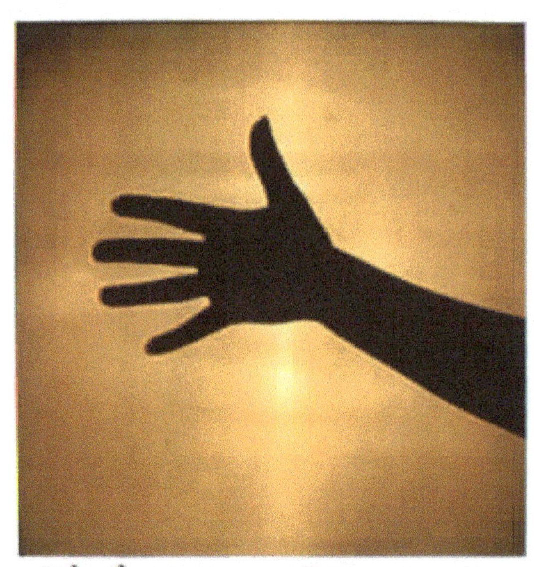

25/5/2008 1^{20}pm.
Her Arm Silhouette

Dear Diary -
The warmth of the glowing light
is interrupted
the beauty of the scene
shifts subtly to infinity,
startled into glorious awareness,
drowning in all that it means
to be
confronted
and visually caressed
by the silhouette of
her arm...

A Vlexicon for Times of War

Thu, 2010/05/06 - 14:37

Monosyllabic
It describes
Time versus frequency
The histogram
Of history
(Read between the lines
Written in invisible blood)

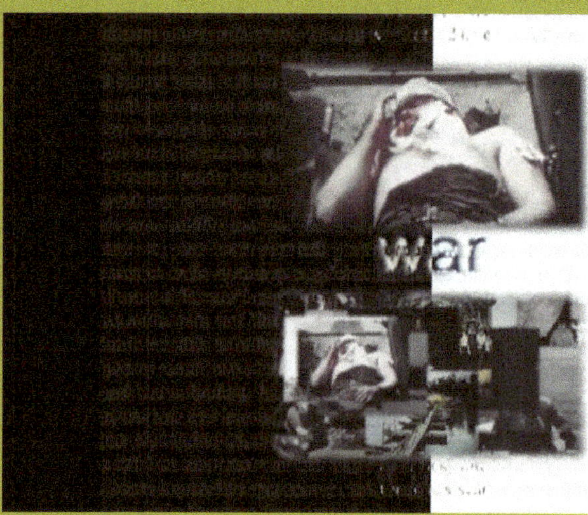

One juncture
(Defined in a three letter word)
Spawns
A glut
Of tasteless gruel
To feed
The masses
And assuage the guilt
Of those who
Accomplish

We Sleep and Dream in Tele-Vision

Thu, 2010/05/06 - 11:01

We sleep
And dream
In tele-vision

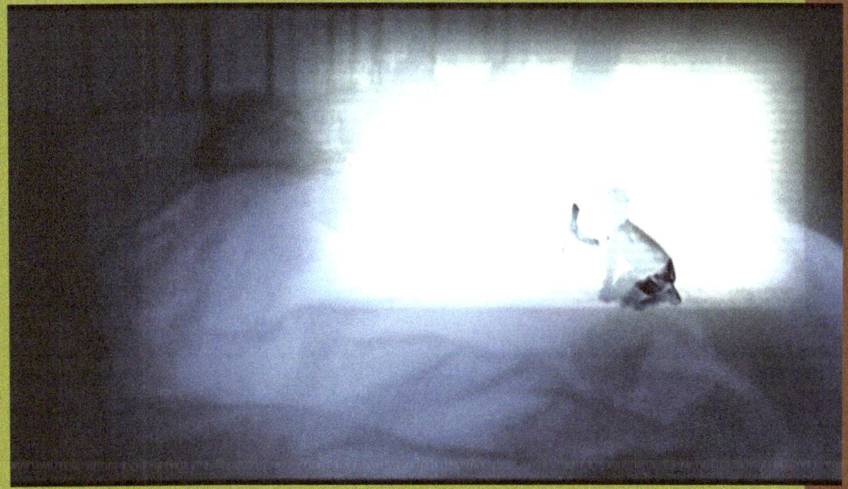

Somnambulant
Wanderings
Through the
Penumbral realms
Of
Our Cimmerian
Landscape

Crepuscular ambience
Invades the aphotic depths
Of our dreaming
Filtered and transubstantiated
By the catalyst
Of one small window

All evil has become
The evening news
Our nightmares
The headlines
Of the day

We sleep
And dream
In tele-vision

Drop TV

(https://youtu.be/GJp6TT9oAO0)

Fri, 2010/04/30 - 13:12

Step carefully
Overhead
Tenuous
And
Invisible threads
Each play chicken
With their breaking point
Over extending
Their failing grasp
On
Damocles' TVs

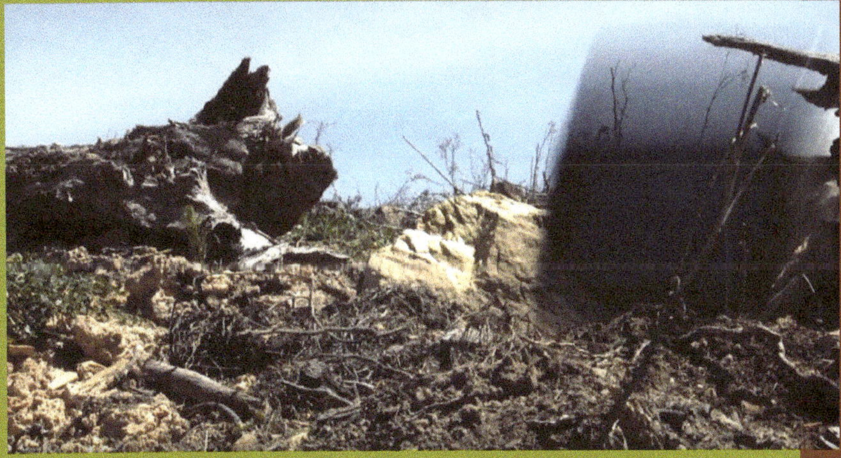

Random
Unpredictable departures
Plummeting
Solid and realised

Shadow and Mass
Violently kiss
Their inevitable junction
Decreed collision
Predetermined
By gravity

You are marked
For
Maximum impact
At
Terminal velocity...

Tuesday Apocalypse

Sat, 2019/01/26 - 16:25

Tuesday
I can be found
Floating in a pool
Clear and perfect blue
As is the sky I see above
Framed by green of palms
I join nature
In worship of the sun
And bask
Warm and languid in its benevolence

Here
There is bliss
And wilful ignorance
Of this world's
Metastasis

Armageddon
Reclines
Relaxed and languorous
On the nearest banana lounge
And smiles

A Painting

(recalling the making of the work [2010 - 2012])

(i) Remembering the occasion

Memory is a perception of my participation
In the truth of what occurred –
Assemblance of a semblance of what was.
I look back, grasping truths
Reframed by the recollection of my
histories:
I seek clarity and answers.

Complete parity eludes my attempts
                to recreate the circumstances
Contained within the mysteries;
Immersions interact, enclasping and
          enmeshing rewards and reproofs.
On balance, a resemblance of cause
Is gathered and transmutes into a
                    concoction of words
Defining the inception and anticipation.

(ii) The persistence of internal dialogue

2010

Two thousand and ten –
I am fifty-two years old and find
myself still encumbered
With a lifetime of baggage.
One would have thought that by now I
would have thrown it out
And continued the journey

With some carry on essentials and a
passport of my true identity.
Credentials of the artist withheld inside me
Are written in each sinew of my being;
in the yearning
Is wrought what I have known in doubt.
A lifeline appears, "*Tibi ipsi esto fidelis*",
the age-old adage –
Golden and distilled, the wonder
Of its truth surrounds and forces me
to consider who I am once again.

(iii) Review and revision in search of essence – self

I have been reincarnated a multitude
of times within this one lifetime
By self and circumstance –
Composer, poet, painter, performer,
teacher, student, husband, father,
lover, preacher –
But always "artist"
Remains the core desire and the best
translation of who I am
And who I am to be.

A decade or two are spanned
(or maybe nearly three).
Containing the fire, I plan
The rut of coming days –
it manifests as darkness.
I know it is featured
With all hope shelved. All purpose and
plans will drift with chance
Except painting be my life line.

(iv) Review and revision in search of essence – the artwork

And so I paint...
My goal is to embody the pleasure of
thinking back on the events
At the end of a perfect day
In the anticipation that the truth
contained within the experience
Will escape the canvas
With each viewing, and consolidate
my spirit with renewal and hope.

In doing I uncover the scope
To distil the primary event;
communicate its essence;
take unforeseen chances.
Illumination and luminescence
Find convergence in the
concrete and abstract;
introspection and play
Enfold. Linking with intent
My hands respond to previously
unknown revelations –
to paint and repaint.

(v) Phenomenology of the occasion

Fidelity to the phenomenon as
it was lived is reshaped by distance
But memory retains
The fundamental elements of this event
that asserts its presence
into my history.
There is place –
Safe, uninterrupted,
a space of my making that
I hold in ownership.
Easel, canvas, brushes and oils;

Peace is tangible. Ideas converge.
I am unrushed as time passes
amidst the turmoils
Of our fate. Alone, I slip
To where the ambience of
the colours and shapes
hold truth within
their embrace.
Wonderment and mystery –
The inherent dynamic and energy of the
original event is captured
and contained
In analogy – the painted instance.

(vi) The aftermath

The artwork persists –
Although complete, it continues
to resonate with the impact
of new revelations
At each new viewing.
In the course of creation,
I become bound to honour
a contract of verbal expression
That evolves and accrues
With each new accord of
colour and tone;
rhythm and stroke;
intention and mark –

To record the essential spark
Involved in my experience of the process,
the product and subsequent views;
The source of words of intercession
That breach the superficial hues;
disclosing truth –
imbuing and renewing.
And so, replete full through
with inspiration
The path is walked... I paint... I edit...
I write... five days in total
and finally it exists.

www.ingramcontent.com/pod-product-compliance
Ingram Content Group UK Ltd.
Pitfield, Milton Keynes, MK11 3LW, UK
UKHW062300290726
14090UKWH00017B/811

9 780645 077728